Turn Trauma into Triumph

Start your Hands-on Journey to Wholeness

Table of content

Dedication

Dedicated to all going through trauma. Do not give up hope. There is victory at the end of the road. I hope this book will give you the encouragement and tools to help you turn the trauma into triumph one day at a time!

Introduction
Understanding Trauma

What is Trauma?

In this chapter, explores the prevalence and impact of trauma on individuals' lives. We'll discuss various forms of trauma and their effects on mental, emotional, and physical well-being. Through practical exercises and real-life examples, readers will gain insight into how to recognize and acknowledge trauma in their own lives.

Understanding Trauma

Trauma is any experience that overwhelms an individual's ability to cope and leaves a lasting impact on their sense of safety, security, and well-being.

There are different types of trauma, including childhood trauma, interpersonal trauma, and community trauma. Provide examples of each to help readers identify potential sources of trauma in their own lives.

Childhood Trauma:

Childhood trauma refers to experiences that occur during childhood or adolescence that are emotionally or physically harmful and have lasting effects.

Examples include:

- o *Physical abuse:* Being physically harmed or injured by a caregiver or authority figure.
- o *Emotional neglect:* Not receiving adequate emotional support or care from caregivers.
- o *Sexual abuse*: Being subjected to unwanted sexual contact or advances.
- o *Witnessing domestic violence:* Seeing one parent or caregiver being abused by another.

Interpersonal Trauma:

Interpersonal trauma occurs within relationships and interactions with others. *Examples include:*

- o *Intimate partner violence:* Suffering physical, emotional, or sexual abuse from a romantic partner.
- o *Bullying:* Enduring repeated aggression, harassment, or exclusion from peers.
- o *Betrayal trauma:* Experiencing trauma as a result of betrayal by a trusted person, such as infidelity in a relationship or deception by a close friend.

o *Workplace harassment:* Being subjected to discrimination, bullying, or harassment by colleagues or superiors.

Community Trauma:
Community trauma arises from events or conditions within a community or society at large.

Examples include:

o *Natural disasters:* Living through events like earthquakes, hurricanes, or floods that cause widespread destruction and loss.

o *Acts of terrorism:* Witnessing or experiencing violence or destruction perpetrated by individuals or groups for ideological reasons.

o *Systemic oppression:* Enduring discrimination, marginalization, or violence due to factors such as race, ethnicity, gender, or sexual orientation.

o *Mass shootings:* Being present during or affected by shootings in public spaces, schools, or workplaces.

Complex Trauma:

Complex trauma refers to exposure to multiple traumatic events, often of an interpersonal nature, over an extended period, and within the context of a relationship where there is an expectation of trust or caregiving.

Examples include:

- o Prolonged exposure to domestic violence or abuse in childhood.
- o Growing up in a war-torn region with ongoing violence and instability.
- o Enduring multiple instances of betrayal or abandonment from caregivers or loved ones.

Secondary Trauma:

Secondary trauma, also known as vicarious trauma, occurs when individuals are exposed to the trauma experiences of others, such as clients, patients, or loved ones, and begin to experience symptoms similar to those who directly experienced the trauma.

Examples include:

- o Therapists or healthcare professionals who work with trauma survivors and become emotionally affected by their stories.
- o Family members or friends who support and care for someone who has experienced a traumatic event and begin to experience symptoms of trauma themselves.

Intergenerational Trauma:

Intergenerational trauma refers to trauma that is passed down from one generation to the next through familial or cultural channels.

Examples include:

- o Descendants of Holocaust survivors experiencing psychological distress or symptoms related to the trauma experienced by their ancestors.
- o Indigenous communities impacted by historical events such as colonization, forced relocation, or cultural genocide, which continue to affect subsequent generations.
- o Descendants of slaves also experience intergenerational trauma.

Medical Trauma:

Medical trauma refers to experiences of distress or harm related to medical treatment, procedures, or diagnoses.

Examples include:

- o Trauma resulting from invasive medical procedures, surgeries, or treatments that cause physical pain or distress.
- o Emotional trauma stemming from receiving a serious medical diagnosis, such as cancer or a chronic illness.

o   Trauma related to experiences in medical settings, such as being in an intensive care unit or witnessing traumatic events in a hospital environment.

Traumatic Grief:

Traumatic grief occurs when an individual experiences the death of a loved one in a sudden, unexpected, or violent manner, leading to intense and prolonged grief reactions intertwined with trauma symptoms.

Examples include:

o   Losing a loved one to suicide, homicide, or a fatal accident.

o   Experiencing the sudden and unexpected death of a child or a close family member.

o   Witnessing the traumatic death of a loved one, such as in a car crash or during a natural disaster.

Identifying potential sources of trauma in one's own life involves reflecting on past experiences and considering how they may have impacted emotional well-being and behavior. Seeking support from mental health professionals can also help individuals recognize and address trauma-related issues. In this book we will delve into a few of the trauma types that are most common.

Recognizing Trauma - Signs and symptoms

Experiencing trauma can have profound effects on an individual's mental, emotional, and physical well-being. Recognizing the signs and symptoms of trauma is crucial for understanding and addressing its impact. Common signs and symptoms of trauma include:

- o *Flashbacks:* Trauma survivors may experience vivid and distressing memories of the traumatic event, often feeling as if they are reliving it. These flashbacks can be triggered by reminders of the trauma and can lead to intense emotional and physical reactions.

- o Hypervigilance: Individuals may develop a heightened state of alertness and sensitivity to potential threats, constantly scanning their environment for danger. This hypervigilance can lead to difficulty relaxing, sleeping disturbances, and a sense of being constantly on edge.

- o *Avoidance Behaviors:* Trauma survivors may go to great lengths to avoid reminders of the traumatic event, including places, people, or activities associated with it. They may also avoid discussing the trauma or seeking help, which can hinder the healing process.

- o *Emotional Numbing:* Some individuals may experience a numbing of emotions as a way to cope with overwhelming feelings of fear, sadness, or anger associated with the trauma. This emotional numbness can manifest as feeling disconnected from oneself or others or experiencing a lack of joy or pleasure in activities once enjoyed.

o Emotional Dysregulation: Trauma survivors may struggle to regulate their emotions, experiencing intense mood swings, irritability, or emotional outbursts disproportionate to the current situation. They may also have difficulty identifying and expressing their emotions accurately.

o *Physical Symptoms:* Trauma can manifest in physical symptoms such as headaches, stomachaches, muscle tension, or other somatic complaints. These physical symptoms may not have a clear medical cause but can be related to the body's physiological response to stress and trauma.

o *Difficulty Trusting Others:* Trauma can erode trust in others, leading to difficulty forming or maintaining relationships. Trauma survivors may have a heightened sense of mistrust, fearing betrayal or abandonment, and may withdraw from social interactions as a result.

o *Negative Self-Image:* Trauma can profoundly impact one's self-perception and self-worth. Survivors may develop negative beliefs about themselves, feeling unworthy, ashamed, or undeserving of love and happiness. These negative self-perceptions can contribute to feelings of hopelessness and low self-esteem.

Recognizing these signs and symptoms is the first step towards healing from trauma. Readers are encouraged to reflect on their own experiences and identify any patterns or symptoms that may indicate unresolved trauma. Seeking support from mental health professionals or support groups can provide validation, understanding, and guidance in addressing trauma and moving towards healing and recovery. It's essential to remember that healing is possible, and reaching out for help is a courageous step towards healing and reclaiming one's well-being.

Trauma triggers:

Trauma triggers are events, situations, or stimuli that evoke memories, emotions, or physical sensations associated with past traumatic experiences. These triggers can be subtle or overt, and encountering them may lead to a range of responses, from mild discomfort to intense distress or even re-experiencing the trauma. Identifying and understanding one's triggers is essential for managing the impact of trauma on daily life and fostering healing and resilience. (see Worksheet VII for Identifying and Managing Trauma Triggers).

Identify Triggers:

Take some time to reflect on past traumatic experiences and consider what specific events, situations, or stimuli tend to evoke memories or emotions associated with those experiences. Common triggers include certain sounds or smells, specific locations, anniversaries of the traumatic event, or interactions with certain people.

Trauma responses:

Trauma responses are automatic reactions that individuals may experience when confronted with a perceived threat or reminder of a traumatic event. Common trauma responses include fight, flight, freeze, and fawn, each of which serves as a survival mechanism in the face of danger. Understanding these responses and their impact on daily functioning is essential for developing healthier coping mechanisms and fostering healing.

Fight:
The fight response involves reacting to a threat by confronting or attacking it. This can manifest as aggression, anger, or defiance. Individuals who exhibit a fight response may become argumentative, defensive, or confrontational when triggered. While this response can sometimes be adaptive in dangerous

situations, it can also lead to interpersonal conflict or escalation of violence.

Flight:
The flight response involves seeking to escape or avoid the perceived threat. This can manifest as avoidance behaviors, such as withdrawing from social interactions, avoiding certain places or activities, or distracting oneself from distressing thoughts or emotions. While flight can help individuals temporarily distance themselves from the source of their distress, it may also lead to isolation, disconnection, or the development of unhealthy coping mechanisms such as substance abuse or compulsive behaviors.

Freeze:
The freeze response involves becoming immobilized or paralyzed in the face of danger. This can manifest as a sense of numbness, dissociation, or feeling "stuck" in a state of fear or helplessness. Individuals who experience a freeze response may feel emotionally disconnected from themselves or their surroundings, making it difficult to engage in daily activities or make decisions.

Fawn:
The fawn response involves seeking to appease or please others as a way to avoid conflict or gain a sense of safety. This can manifest as people-pleasing behaviors, such as being overly accommodating, submissive, or compliant in relationships.

While fawning can help individuals navigate threatening situations by seeking to avoid harm, it can also lead to boundary violations, codependency, or a loss of autonomy.

By increasing awareness of your trauma responses and developing healthier coping mechanisms, you can empower yourself to navigate triggers more effectively and cultivate greater resilience and well-being in your daily life. Remember that healing is a journey, and it's okay to seek professional support if needed.

Acknowledging Trauma

Breaking the silence: Emphasize the importance of acknowledging and validating one's own trauma experiences, even if they may feel uncomfortable or overwhelming. Provide journal prompts or guided reflections to help readers explore their feelings and experiences in a safe and supportive way.

Acknowledging trauma is a crucial step in the healing process, yet it can be challenging due to feelings of shame, fear, or disbelief. Breaking the silence and validating one's own trauma experiences is essential for reclaiming personal agency and fostering resilience. Here's how readers can begin this journey:

Validate Your Experience: Remind yourself that your feelings and experiences are valid, even if they may be difficult to acknowledge. Denying or minimizing your trauma only prolongs the healing process.

Understand the Impact: Recognize how trauma has affected various aspects of your life, including your emotions, relationships, and overall well-being. Acknowledging the impact of trauma is the first step towards healing.

Break the Silence: Challenge the silence surrounding your trauma by giving yourself permission to speak openly and honestly about your experiences. Share your story with trusted individuals who can offer support and validation.

Seek support: Reaching out to trusted friends, family members, or professionals for support and validation. Find trauma-informed therapists or support groups where they can connect with others who have similar experiences in your area. We explore some of these action points further in coming chapters.

In this chapter, we've explored the prevalence and impact of trauma on individuals' lives. By understanding the signs and symptoms of trauma, recognizing triggers and responses, and acknowledging their own experiences, readers can take the first steps toward healing and reclaiming their well-being.

The Science of Trauma

In this chapter, we'll delve into the neuroscience behind trauma, exploring how traumatic experiences affect the brain, stress response systems, and overall health. Through easy-to-understand explanations, practical exercises, and real-life examples, readers will gain insight into the physiological mechanisms underlying trauma and its effects on the body and mind.

The Brain and Trauma

Brain regions involved: Trauma can have profound effects on the brain, particularly in areas involved in processing emotions,

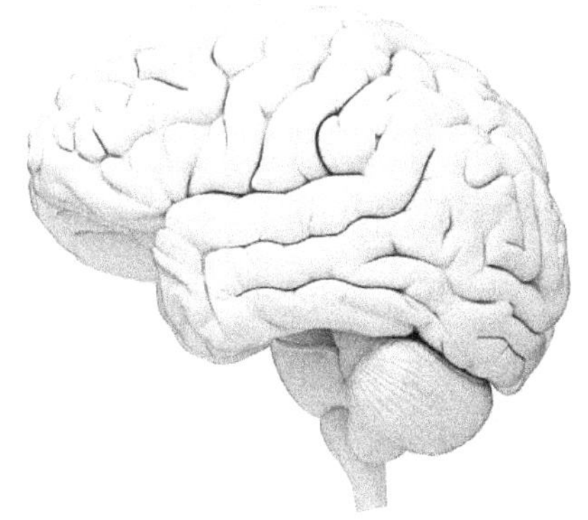

memories, and stress responses. Three key brain areas often implicated in trauma are the amygdala, hippocampus, and prefrontal cortex.

The amygdala plays a central role in the brain's emotional processing and response to threats. When trauma occurs, the amygdala can become hyperactive, leading to heightened emotional arousal and a hypersensitive threat detection system.

Dysregulation of the amygdala can result in symptoms such as hypervigilance, where individuals are constantly on high alert for potential danger. This heightened state of arousal can lead to an exaggerated startle response, increased anxiety, and difficulty relaxing or feeling safe in one's environment.

The hippocampus is involved in the formation and consolidation of memories, particularly contextual and episodic memories. During a traumatic event, the hippocampus may be overwhelmed by the intense emotional and sensory input, impairing its ability to encode and store memories effectively.

As a result, trauma survivors may experience fragmented or disjointed memories of the traumatic event, making it difficult to integrate and make sense of their experiences. This can contribute to symptoms such as flashbacks, where intrusive memories of the trauma are re-experienced as if they are happening in the present moment.

The prefrontal cortex, particularly the ventromedial prefrontal cortex (vmPFC), is responsible for higher-order cognitive functions such as decision-making, impulse control, and emotion regulation. It also plays a crucial role in modulating the stress response and regulating emotional reactivity.

In response to trauma, the prefrontal cortex may become dysregulated, leading to difficulties in regulating emotions and controlling impulsive behaviors. This can manifest as emotional dysregulation, where individuals may experience intense mood swings, irritability, or difficulty managing their reactions to stressors.

Overall, dysregulation of the amygdala, hippocampus, and prefrontal cortex can contribute to a range of symptoms commonly associated with trauma, including hypervigilance, flashbacks, and emotional dysregulation. Understanding the neurobiological underpinnings of these symptoms can help inform trauma-informed interventions and treatments aimed at restoring balance and promoting healing in the brain.

Neuroplasticity:

An interesting concept to know is Neuroplasticity, which refers to the brain's remarkable ability to reorganize itself by forming new neural connections and pathways throughout life in response to experiences, learning, and environmental changes.

This concept highlights the brain's dynamic nature and its capacity for adaptation and growth.

When it comes to trauma, neuroplasticity plays a significant role in shaping the brain's response to adverse experiences. Trauma can alter neural pathways and synaptic connections in both negative and positive ways, depending on various factors such as the nature of the trauma, the timing of exposure, and the availability of supportive interventions.

Therapy and Support: such as cognitive-behavioral therapy, Eye Movement Desensitization and Reprocessing, and mindfulness-based interventions, can help individuals process and integrate traumatic memories.

Social Support: Strong social connections and supportive relationships can buffer the effects of trauma on the brain.

Lifestyle Factors: such as regular exercise, adequate sleep, nutritious diet, and stress management techniques, can support neuroplasticity and resilience in the face of trauma.

Chronic Stress: Traumatic experiences can trigger the release of stress hormones such as cortisol, which can have detrimental effects on the brain over time.

Dysregulation of Neural Circuits: Trauma can disrupt the balance and function of neural circuits involved in processing emotions, stress responses, and threat detection.

Altered Neurotransmission: Trauma can affect neurotransmitter systems in the brain, such as serotonin and dopamine, which play key roles in mood regulation and reward processing.

Stress Response Systems

Stress response systems are physiological mechanisms that enable the body to respond to perceived threats or stressors. Two key components of the stress response system are the fight-or-flight response and the hypothalamic-pituitary-adrenal (HPA) axis.

Fight-or-Flight Response:

The fight-or-flight response is an innate survival mechanism that prepares the body to either confront a threat (fight) or flee from it (flight). When triggered, the sympathetic nervous system activates, leading to a cascade of physiological changes aimed at increasing alertness and readiness for action.

Physiological Changes: During the fight-or-flight response, several changes occur in the body, including:

- o Increased heart rate and blood pressure to enhance circulation and oxygen delivery to muscles and organs.
- o Rapid breathing to increase oxygen intake and prepare the body for physical exertion.
- o Heightened arousal and vigilance, accompanied by dilated pupils and increased sensory perception.

Release of stress hormones such as adrenaline (epinephrine) and noradrenaline (norepinephrine) from the adrenal glands, which further amplify the body's physiological response to stress.

Dysregulation from Chronic Trauma: Chronic or repeated exposure to trauma can dysregulate the fight-or-flight response, leading to persistent activation of the stress response system. This prolonged state of hyperarousal can result in physical and psychological health consequences, including cardiovascular problems, immune dysfunction, anxiety disorders, and post-traumatic stress disorder (PTSD).

HPA Axis Dysregulation:

The HPA axis is a complex neuroendocrine system involved in the body's response to stress. It comprises the hypothalamus, pituitary gland, and adrenal glands, which work together to regulate the production and release of stress hormones, particularly cortisol.

Role of the HPA Axis: When the brain perceives a stressor, the hypothalamus releases corticotropin-releasing hormone (CRH), which stimulates the pituitary gland to release adrenocorticotropic hormone (ACTH). ACTH, in turn, triggers the adrenal glands to produce and release cortisol, the body's primary stress hormone.

Dysregulation in Trauma: Individuals with a history of trauma may exhibit dysregulation of the HPA axis, leading to alterations in cortisol production and regulation. This dysregulation can manifest as:

Hypersensitivity or blunted responsiveness to stressors.

Irregular cortisol patterns, such as heightened baseline levels or blunted diurnal rhythms.

Impaired feedback mechanisms that regulate cortisol release, leading to chronic elevation or suppression of cortisol levels.

Practical Exercises for Identifying Signs of HPA Axis

Dysregulation and Restoring Balance:

Self-Reflection: Reflect on your stress response patterns and how they may have been influenced by past traumatic experiences. Pay attention to physical and emotional symptoms of stress, such as fatigue, irritability, insomnia, or difficulty concentrating.

Stress Journaling: Keep a journal to track your stress levels and identify triggers that activate your stress response. Notice any patterns or trends in your stress responses over time.

Relaxation Techniques: Practice relaxation techniques such as deep breathing, progressive muscle relaxation, meditation, or yoga to help regulate the stress response and promote relaxation and calm.

Healthy Lifestyle Habits: Prioritize self-care activities such as regular exercise, adequate sleep, nutritious diet, and stress management practices to support the health and balance of the HPA axis.

Seek Professional Support: Consider seeking support from a therapist or healthcare provider who specializes in trauma-informed care. They can help you explore strategies for managing stress and restoring balance to the HPA axis through evidence-based interventions and therapeutic techniques.

By understanding the physiological mechanisms of the stress response system and recognizing signs of dysregulation, individuals can empower themselves to implement effective strategies for managing stress, promoting resilience, and supporting overall well-being, particularly in the context of trauma histories.

Trauma and Physical Health

Trauma can have profound effects on physical health, with research indicating strong connections between trauma exposure and various medical conditions. Understanding these links and incorporating holistic approaches to physical healing can be crucial for trauma survivors in promoting overall well-being.

Impact on Physical Health:

Chronic Pain: Trauma survivors often experience higher rates of chronic pain conditions such as fibromyalgia, headaches, and musculoskeletal pain. Chronic pain can be both a consequence of trauma-induced stress responses and a manifestation of unresolved emotional distress.

Example: Sarah, who experienced childhood abuse, develops chronic back pain as an adult. Despite medical interventions, her pain persists due to underlying trauma-related stress and tension stored in her body.

Autoimmune Disorders:

Trauma has been linked to dysregulation of the immune system, increasing the risk of autoimmune disorders such as rheumatoid arthritis, lupus, and inflammatory bowel disease. Chronic stress and inflammation associated with trauma can exacerbate autoimmune symptoms.

Example: John, who survived a traumatic car accident, later develops rheumatoid arthritis. The ongoing stress from his trauma history contributes to inflammation and immune dysregulation, worsening his autoimmune symptoms.

Cardiovascular Disease:

Trauma exposure is associated with an increased risk of cardiovascular disease, including hypertension, heart disease, and stroke. Chronic activation of the body's stress response system can lead to elevated blood pressure, inflammation, and cardiovascular damage over time.

Example: Maria, who witnessed a traumatic event during military service, develops hypertension and experiences a heart attack in her 50s. Her trauma history contributes to chronic stress and physiological changes that impact her cardiovascular health.

Healing the Body:

Nutrition: Adopting a balanced and nutritious diet can support physical healing and overall well-being. Focus on whole foods rich in nutrients, antioxidants, and anti-inflammatory properties, while minimizing processed foods, sugar, and caffeine.

Exercise: Regular physical activity can help reduce stress, improve mood, and alleviate physical symptoms associated with trauma. Find activities you enjoy, such as walking, yoga, swimming, or dancing, and incorporate them into your routine.

Bodywork: Therapeutic modalities such as massage therapy, acupuncture, and chiropractic care can help release tension, reduce pain, and promote relaxation in the body. Explore different bodywork techniques to find what works best for you.

Alternative Therapies: Consider complementary approaches such as acupuncture, mindfulness meditation, biofeedback, or herbal remedies to support physical healing and stress reduction. Consult with qualified practitioners to explore safe and effective options.

By addressing trauma-related physical health issues through holistic approaches, individuals can support their bodies' natural healing processes and enhance overall well-being. It's essential to prioritize self-care practices that promote physical and emotional healing, recognizing the interconnectedness of mind, body, and spirit in the journey toward recovery from trauma.

In this chapter, we've explored the neuroscience behind trauma and its effects on the brain, stress response systems, and physical health. By understanding the physiological mechanisms underlying trauma, readers can gain insight into their own experiences and explore holistic approaches to healing and well-being.

Part One
Understanding Trauma

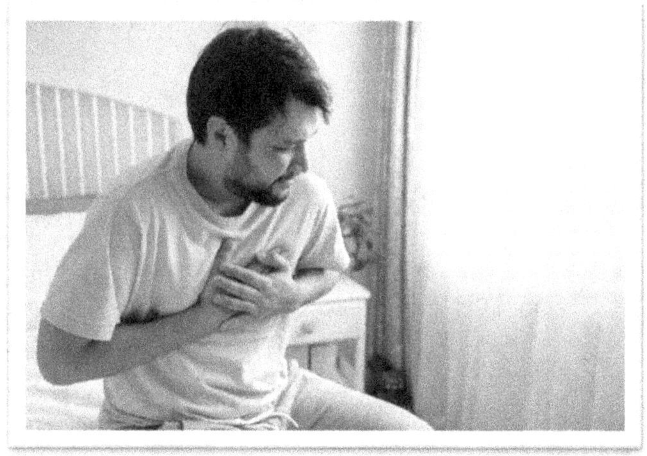

Unraveling the Layers of Trauma

In this chapter, we'll explore practical easy-to-understand exercises, and real-life examples, to help readers gain deeper insight into not just the diverse nature of trauma and its impact on individuals' lives but also how to triumph over trauma.

Childhood Adversity

Childhood adversity or childhood trauma which derives from experiences of abuse, neglect, household dysfunction, and other adverse childhood experiences (ACEs) experienced during child and that have long-lasting effects on individuals' development and well-being. These traumas can include physical abuse, sexual abuse, emotional abuse, neglect, and household dysfunction (e.g., parental substance abuse, domestic violence, mental illness).

Such trauma often has lasting effects on individuals' mental,

emotional, and physical health, such as increased risk of mental health disorders, substance abuse, relationship difficulties, and chronic health conditions. Below are some practical exercises you can do to combat trauma.

Practical Exercises:

Reflect on your own childhood experiences and identify any adverse experiences or traumas you may have encountered. For this we will the ACEs questionnaire or journal prompts to explore how these experiences may have impacted your life and well-being.

ACEs Questionnaire:

The ACEs questionnaire is a tool used to assess the prevalence and impact of adverse childhood experiences (ACEs) on individuals' lives. It typically consists of a series of questions that inquire about specific types of childhood trauma or adversity that an individual may have experienced. Each question is scored, and the total score indicates the individual's level of exposure to ACEs.

ACEs Questions	SCORE	
	Yes	No
Before the age of 18, did a parent or other adult in the household often or very often swear at you, insult you, put you down, or humiliate you?		
Before the age of 18, did a parent or other adult in the household often or very often push, grab, slap, or throw something at you?		
Before the age of 18, did you often or very often feel that no one in your family loved you or thought you were important or special?		

Before the age of 18, did you often or very often feel that you didn't have enough to eat, had to wear dirty clothes, or had no one to protect you?		

Journal Prompts:

Journal prompts are open-ended questions or statements designed to encourage self-reflection and exploration of one's thoughts, feelings, and experiences. They can be used as a tool for individuals to delve deeper into their experiences of trauma or adversity and how these experiences have impacted their lives and well-being.

Examples of journal questions to reflect upon:
Reflect on a significant childhood memory that still resonates with you today. How does this memory make you feel, and what impact has it had on your life?
Journal entry:

Describe a challenging or traumatic experience you faced in childhood. How did you cope with this experience at the time, and how has it shaped your beliefs and behaviors as an adult?
Journal Entry:
Think about the relationships you had with caregivers or family members during your childhood. How did these relationships influence your sense of safety, trust, and belonging?
Journal entry:
Consider the ways in which your childhood experiences have impacted your mental, emotional, and physical health. Are there any patterns or symptoms that you recognize as being related to these experiences?
Journal Entry:

Imagine your ideal vision of healing and well-being. What steps can you take to nurture and support yourself on your healing journey?

Journal Entry:

These journal prompts can serve as starting points for individuals to explore their experiences of trauma or adversity, gain insight into the impact of these experiences on their lives, and begin the process of healing and growth.

My cousin Sarah grew up in a household where her parents frequently fought and her father struggled with alcohol addiction. As a child, she often felt scared and anxious, never knowing when the next outburst would occur. As an adult, Sarah struggles with anxiety and low self-esteem, and she finds it difficult to trust others in relationships. Through therapy and self-reflection, Sarah has begun to recognize how her childhood experiences have shaped her beliefs and behaviors, and she is committed to healing and breaking the cycle of trauma in her own life.

Traumatic Events in Adulthood

Traumatic events in adulthood are another example through which individuals experience trauma. This kind of trauma can encompass a wide range of experiences, including accidents, natural disasters, violence, loss of a loved one, medical trauma, experiences of racism, phobia and/or other life-threatening situations that can have adverse effects on individuals' lives and well-being. Often times, if not checked, these traumatic experiences leave lasting effects on individuals' mental, emotional, and physical health, such as PTSD, depression, anxiety, and somatic symptoms.

Practical Exercise:

Reflect on any traumatic events or significant life challenges you have experienced in adulthood.

Use journal prompts or guided reflections to explore your thoughts, feelings, and reactions to these experiences, as well as any coping strategies you have utilized.

Example:
Former classmate of mine David was involved in a car accident several years ago that left him with physical injuries and emotional trauma. Despite receiving medical treatment and therapy, he continues to struggle with flashbacks, nightmares, and avoidance behaviors related to the accident. Through support from loved ones and therapy, he is learning to cope with his trauma and rebuild his life.

In this chapter, we've explored the different types of trauma that individuals may experience throughout their lives, from childhood adversity to traumatic events in adulthood. By understanding the diverse nature of trauma and its lasting effects on individuals' lives, readers can begin to recognize and address their own trauma experiences, paving the way for healing and growth.

A Scientific Approach to Tackling Trauma

In this chapter, we'll continue to explore the fascinating field of neuroscience to understand how trauma affects the brain, stress response systems, and overall health. We'll delve into the physiological mechanisms underlying trauma and its effects on individuals' mental, emotional, and physical well-being. Through easy-to-understand explanations, practical exercises, and real-life examples, readers will gain insight into the science behind trauma and its profound impact on the body and mind.

Understanding Brain Function

In chapter two we looked briefly at the brain and its functions in a bid to gain an overview of the brain's structure and functions, highlighting key regions involved in processing emotions, regulating stress responses, and forming memories.

We learnt how traumatic experiences can disrupt normal brain function, particularly in areas such as the amygdala (responsible for processing emotions and fear responses), hippocampus (involved in memory formation and retrieval), and prefrontal cortex (responsible for decision-making and impulse control). Below are some exercises to help deepen that knowledge and work towards combating neurological trauma.

Practical Exercises:

Brain Mapping Activity

Below is a simple diagram of the brain, can you label the key regions mentioned in the earlier chapter? While doing so, please I wish to encourage you to Reflect on how trauma may affect each region and its associated functions.

Lable the 3 key regions of the brain in diagram below:

Reflect, below on how trauma may affect each region and its associated functions:

Amygdala:

Hippocampus:

Prefrontal cortex:

Stress Response Systems

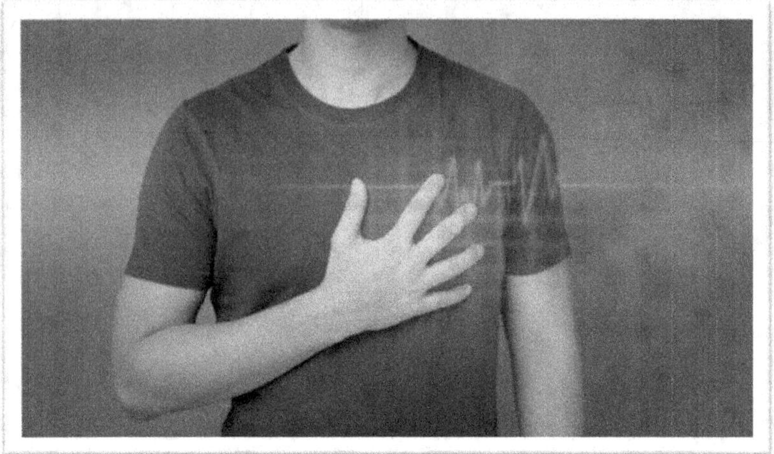

Earlier on, we saw how the body's natural response to stress, known as the fight-or-flight response, is a physiological reaction that occurs when an individual perceives a threat. This response is designed to prepare the body to either fight the threat or flee from it. The process is initiated by the hypothalamus in the brain, which activates the sympathetic nervous system and triggers the release of stress hormones such as adrenaline and cortisol

When that happens, Adrenaline (epinephrine) is rapidly released into the bloodstream, causing an immediate increase in heart rate, blood pressure, and energy supplies. It enhances alertness, sharpens focus, and readies muscles for action.

Cortisol is released slightly later and plays a key role in maintaining prolonged alertness. It increases glucose in the bloodstream, enhances the brain's use of glucose, and curbs non-essential functions in a fight-or-flight situation, such as immune responses and digestion.

These hormonal changes collectively ensure that the body is primed to respond to the immediate threat effectively.

Consequences of a stressed Response system after a traumatic experience

Dysregulation of Stress Response Systems:

Now, when an individual experiences trauma, it can dysregulate the body's stress response systems, leading to several detrimental effects:

Hyperarousal: This is a state of increased psychological and physiological tension marked by heightened awareness and sensitivity to stimuli. Individuals may experience difficulty sleeping, irritability, and an exaggerated startle response.

Hypervigilance: In this state, a person remains excessively alert and watchful for potential threats. This constant state of alertness can lead to anxiety, fatigue, and difficulty concentrating.

Chronic Activation: Prolonged exposure to stressors or trauma can result in the chronic activation of the stress response system. This can cause continuous elevation of cortisol and adrenaline levels, which can have harmful effects on the body, including impaired immune function, increased risk of cardiovascular disease, and mental health disorders like anxiety and depression.

Trauma-induced dysregulation of the stress response systems can therefore lead to significant long-term health issues, both physical and psychological, due to the body's inability to properly manage and mitigate stress.

Practical Exercise

Stress Response Inventory

Please a checklist of common stress response symptoms. Try to identify which symptoms you experience most frequently. On the right-side column, try to reflect on how these symptoms may be related to their experiences of trauma.

Common symptoms	How does symptom relate to your experience of trauma?
Increased heart rate	

Muscle tension or tightness	
Difficulty sleeping or insomnia	
Changes in appetite (eating too much or too little)	
Fatigue or low energy levels	
Irritability or mood swings	
Racing thoughts or difficulty concentrating	
Hypervigilance or heightened awareness of surroundings	
Avoidance behaviors (avoiding certain places, people, or activities)	
Flashbacks or intrusive memories	
Panic attacks or feelings of impending doom	
Nausea or gastrointestinal distress	
Excessive sweating	

Feeling overwhelmed or easily startled	
Emotional numbness or detachment	

In addition to the exercise above, we suggest seeking support from a mental health professional if you find that these symptoms significantly impact your daily functioning or quality of life.

Impact on Overall Health

Mental Health Effects: Explore the link between trauma and mental health disorders such as PTSD, depression, and anxiety, discussing how trauma can affect mood, cognition, and behavior.

Physical Health Effects: Discuss the impact of trauma on physical health, including increased risk of chronic health conditions such as heart disease, autoimmune disorders, and gastrointestinal problems.

Practical Exercise: Health Impact Journal

In this journal template below, you'll find a structured way to track your mental and physical health symptoms over time. By keeping a record of your experiences, you can begin to notice patterns and correlations between trauma and your health symptoms. Understanding these connections can provide valuable insight into your own well-being and guide you towards holistic approaches to healing.

Instructions:

- o Fill out the journal entries daily, noting any relevant symptoms or experiences.
- o Reflect on your entries periodically to identify patterns or correlations between trauma and your health symptoms.
- o Use this journal as a tool for self-awareness and exploration on your journey towards healing and well-being.

Journal template
Date:..
Time:..

Location:..
....

Physical Health Symptoms:

Headaches:...
....

Muscle tension:

....
....

Fatigue:..
....

Digestive issues:

....
....

Sleep disturbances:

....
....

Appetite changes:

....
....

Other:..
....

Mental Health Symptoms:

Anxiety:..

....

Depression:...

....

Flashbacks:...

....

Nightmares:..

....

Irritability:...

....

Mood swings:

....

....

Difficulty concentrating:

....

....

Other:...

....

Trauma Triggers or Stressors:

Specific events or memories:

....

Certain environments or situations

:..

....

Interpersonal conflicts:

....

Work or academic stress:

....

....

Other:..

....

Coping Strategies:

....

....

Deep breathing exercises

Meditation or mindfulness:

....

Physical activity:

....

....

Creative expression (e.g., writing, art):

....

....

Seeking social support:

....

....

.

Therapy or counseling:

....

....

Other:..

....

Reflections:

Are there any patterns or correlations between your experiences of trauma and your health symptoms?

....

....

....

....

....

How do your coping strategies impact your overall well-being?

....

....

....

....

....

What insights have you gained from tracking your symptoms over time?

....

....

....

....

....

Additional Notes:

....

....

....

....

....

Remember, this journal is a tool for self-awareness and exploration. Be gentle with yourself as you navigate your journey towards healing and well-being. If you find it challenging to cope with your symptoms or need additional support, consider reaching out to a therapist or mental health professional for assistance.

By understanding the neuroscience behind trauma and its effects on your brain and body, you're taking an important step towards reclaiming your health and vitality. Stay committed to your healing journey and remember that you are not alone.

In this chapter, we've explored the neuroscience behind trauma and its effects on brain function, stress response systems, and overall health. By understanding the physiological mechanisms underlying trauma, readers can gain insight into their own experiences and begin to explore holistic approaches to healing and well-being.

Part Two

Awareness and Resilience

– The Often Ignored Tools

Cultivating Awareness

In this chapter, we will explore further (introduced in chapter one) the crucial first step in the healing journey: cultivating awareness of our own trauma. Recognizing and acknowledging our experiences of trauma is essential for initiating the process of healing. By becoming aware of how trauma has impacted us, we can begin to take proactive steps towards healing and reclaiming our well-being. Below, you will find some exercises that can help you raise awareness about your trauma.

Exercise 1: Mindful Body Scan

Begin by finding a quiet and comfortable space where you can relax without distractions. Close your eyes and take a few deep breaths to center yourself. Start by bringing your attention to your feet and slowly scan your body from the bottom up, noticing any sensations or areas of tension. Pay attention to any areas that feel uncomfortable or tense, and gently breathe into them, allowing them to soften and relax. This practice can help you become more attuned to the physical manifestations of trauma in your body.

Example: As you scan your body, you may notice tightness in your chest or knots in your stomach. These physical sensations could be indicative of underlying emotional distress related to past trauma. By acknowledging these sensations, you are taking the first step towards understanding and addressing the impact of trauma on your body.

Exercise 2: Journaling Prompts

Take some time to reflect on your experiences of trauma through journaling. Here are some prompts to guide your reflection:

- o Describe a specific event or memory that you believe has contributed to your trauma.
- o How did you feel during and after the traumatic event? What emotions come up for you when you think about it now?
- o How has the trauma affected various aspects of your life, such as relationships, work, or daily functioning?
- o What coping mechanisms have you used to deal with the trauma? Are there any patterns or behaviors that you notice?
- o What are your hopes and intentions for healing and recovery?

Example: You might write about a car accident you were involved in and how it left you feeling anxious and on edge whenever you have to drive. Reflecting on how this trauma has impacted your daily life can help you recognize the extent of its influence and motivate you to seek support and healing.

Exercise 3: Identifying Triggers

Start paying attention to situations, people, or events that trigger feelings of distress or anxiety for you. Keep a journal or make a mental note of these triggers and any physical or emotional reactions they elicit. By identifying your triggers, you can begin to understand the specific aspects of your trauma that still affect you and develop strategies for managing them.

Example: You might notice that loud noises trigger feelings of panic and hypervigilance, reminding you of a traumatic experience where you felt unsafe. Recognizing this trigger allows you to take steps to mitigate its impact, such as using noise-canceling headphones or practicing grounding techniques when you encounter loud noises.

Cultivating awareness of our own trauma is a vital step towards healing and well-being. By practicing mindfulness, journaling, and identifying triggers, we can begin to unravel the complex layers of our trauma and take proactive steps towards healing. Remember to be patient and compassionate with yourself as you embark on this journey of self-discovery and healing.

Embracing Resilience

In this chapter, we delve into the profound concept of resilience—a fundamental attribute that empowers individuals to rebound from adversity and flourish despite challenging circumstances. By understanding and harnessing our resilience, we not only navigate the journey of healing from trauma but also emerge stronger and more resilient than before.

Understanding Resilience:

Resilience is not merely about enduring or deflecting trauma; rather, it involves acknowledging the impact of adversity while finding ways to adapt, grow, and thrive in its aftermath. It requires recognizing the innate strength and resources within ourselves and tapping into external support systems when necessary. Resilience is a dynamic quality that can be cultivated and reinforced through deliberate practice and self-awareness.

Tools and Techniques for Building Resilience

Cultivate Self-Compassion:

Self-compassion is the cornerstone of resilience, allowing us to extend kindness, understanding, and acceptance towards ourselves, particularly during times of distress or hardship. It involves treating ourselves with the same warmth and empathy that we would offer to a cherished friend facing similar challenges. By embracing self-compassion, we create a nurturing inner environment conducive to healing and growth.

Example: Rather than berating yourself for perceived shortcomings or setbacks, practice self-compassion by acknowledging your efforts and acknowledging the inherent humanity in experiencing difficulty. Offer yourself words of encouragement and reassurance, affirming that it's okay to struggle and that you are worthy of compassion and care.

Develop a Growth Mindset:

A growth mindset is the belief that challenges and setbacks are opportunities for learning and personal development rather than insurmountable obstacles. Embracing a growth mindset enables us to view adversity as a natural part of the human experience, capable of fostering resilience and fortitude. By focusing on our capacity for growth and improvement, we can approach challenges with curiosity, resilience, and a sense of possibility.

Example: Instead of interpreting failure as a reflection of your inherent worth or capabilities, adopt a growth mindset by reframing setbacks as valuable learning experiences. Embrace the opportunity to glean insights and lessons from adversity, recognizing that each challenge presents an opportunity for growth and self-discovery.

Build Supportive Relationships:

Strong social connections are essential for bolstering resilience and providing invaluable emotional support during times of distress. Cultivate relationships with friends, family members, or support groups who offer empathy, validation, and encouragement. By surrounding ourselves with a supportive network of individuals who understand and validate our experiences, we mitigate feelings of isolation and foster a sense of belonging and connection.

Example: Seek out opportunities to connect with trusted friends or family members, sharing your thoughts, feelings, and experiences of trauma in a safe and supportive environment. Consider joining a support group or online community comprised of individuals who share similar experiences, providing a forum for mutual support, understanding, and camaraderie.

Cultivate Gratitude:

Practicing gratitude involves intentionally focusing on the positive aspects of our lives, even amidst adversity. By cultivating an attitude of gratitude, we shift our perspective towards abundance and resilience, fostering a sense of hope and optimism. Regularly take time to reflect on the blessings, joys, and small victories in your life, no matter how insignificant they may seem. Keeping a gratitude journal or simply pausing to appreciate the beauty and goodness around you can cultivate resilience and fortify your emotional well-being.

Example: At the end of each day, make a habit of identifying three things you are grateful for, whether it's a supportive friend, a moment of laughter, or a beautiful sunset. By actively acknowledging the positive elements in your life, you cultivate resilience and foster a sense of gratitude and contentment.

Set Boundaries and Prioritize Self-Care:

Setting healthy boundaries and prioritizing self-care are essential practices for preserving your emotional, physical, and mental well-being, particularly in the aftermath of trauma. Learn to recognize your own limits and honor your needs, whether it's taking breaks when you feel overwhelmed, saying no to additional responsibilities, or seeking professional support when necessary. Engage in activities that nourish and replenish your spirit, such as exercise, hobbies, spending time in nature, or practicing relaxation techniques. By prioritizing self-care and setting boundaries, you replenish your inner resources and enhance your resilience in the face of adversity.

Example: Schedule regular self-care activities into your daily or weekly routine, whether it's going for a walk in nature, enjoying a soothing bath, or indulging in your favorite hobby. Honor your need for rest, relaxation, and rejuvenation, recognizing that self-care is not selfish but essential for cultivating resilience and well-being.

Foster Adaptive Coping Strategies:

Explore and cultivate adaptive coping strategies that promote resilience and enhance your ability to navigate challenges effectively. Adaptive coping strategies focus on problem-solving, emotional regulation, and seeking support from others, rather than relying on avoidance or maladaptive coping mechanisms. Experiment with different coping techniques such as cognitive reframing, seeking social support, engaging in creative expression, or practicing relaxation techniques. Identify the coping strategies that resonate most with you and integrate them into your daily life as tools for building resilience and managing stress.

Example: When faced with a challenging situation or triggering event, practice cognitive reframing by consciously shifting your perspective to focus on opportunities for growth and learning. Reach out to a trusted friend or therapist for support and guidance, seeking validation and perspective outside of your own. By fostering adaptive coping strategies, you empower yourself to navigate adversity with resilience, resourcefulness, and grace.

Practice Mindfulness and Stress Management:

Mindfulness practices such as meditation, deep breathing, and yoga serve as potent tools for cultivating resilience and managing stress. Mindfulness involves directing our awareness to the present moment with curiosity and nonjudgment, allowing us to cultivate inner peace, clarity, and resilience in the face of adversity. By incorporating mindfulness into our daily lives, we enhance our capacity to navigate challenges with grace, equanimity, and resilience.

Example: Dedicate time each day to engage in mindfulness practices such as meditation or deep breathing exercises, immersing yourself fully in the present moment and observing any thoughts, emotions, or sensations that arise without judgment or attachment. Notice how practicing mindfulness cultivates a sense of calm, centeredness, and resilience, enabling you to respond to adversity with greater clarity and composure.

Cultivate Flexibility and Adaptability:

Resilience involves the ability to adapt to changing circumstances and navigate uncertainty with flexibility and grace. Cultivate a mindset of flexibility by embracing change as a natural part of life and reframing challenges as opportunities for growth and adaptation. Practice letting go of rigid expectations and embracing the inherent uncertainty of life, recognizing that flexibility allows for resilience to flourish in the face of adversity.

Example: When confronted with unexpected changes or setbacks, approach them with an open mind and a willingness to adapt. Instead of resisting change, ask yourself how you can creatively adapt to new circumstances and find innovative solutions to challenges. By cultivating flexibility and adaptability, you empower yourself to navigate adversity with resilience and resourcefulness.

Engage in Meaning-Making:

Seeking meaning and purpose in the midst of trauma can be a powerful catalyst for resilience and healing. Engage in activities that align with your values, passions, and sense of purpose, allowing you to derive meaning from your experiences and cultivate a sense of resilience and hope. Reflect on how your experiences of trauma have shaped your values, beliefs, and priorities, and explore ways to integrate these insights into your life in meaningful and purposeful ways.

Example: Explore activities or pursuits that bring you a sense of fulfillment and meaning, whether it's volunteering for a cause you're passionate about, pursuing creative expression through art or music, or engaging in spiritual practices that nourish your soul. By actively seeking meaning and purpose in your life, you cultivate resilience and tap into a deep wellspring of inner strength and vitality.

Practice Forgiveness and Letting Go:

Forgiveness is a powerful practice that can facilitate healing and promote resilience in the aftermath of trauma. Practice forgiveness by letting go of resentment, anger, and bitterness towards yourself and others, releasing the emotional burdens that weigh you down and hinder your growth. Recognize that forgiveness is not condoning or excusing the harm inflicted upon you but rather freeing yourself from the grip of past pain and reclaiming your power to heal and thrive.

Example: Reflect on any lingering resentments or grievances you hold towards yourself or others, and consider the possibility of forgiveness as a pathway to liberation and healing. Practice self-compassion and extend forgiveness towards yourself for any perceived shortcomings or mistakes, recognizing that you are worthy of love, compassion, and forgiveness. By cultivating forgiveness and letting go of past hurts, you create space for resilience, healing, and transformation to unfold.

Incorporating these additional tips and practices into your resilience-building toolkit enhances your capacity to navigate the complexities of trauma and adversity with courage, strength, and resilience. Remember that resilience is not about avoiding pain or hardship but rather embracing life's challenges as opportunities for growth, learning, and transformation. With each intentional practice and mindful choice, you strengthen your resilience and move forward on the path to healing, wholeness, and flourishing.

Embracing resilience is a transformative journey of self-discovery, growth, and empowerment—an unwavering testament to the indomitable human spirit. By cultivating self-compassion, fostering a growth mindset, nurturing supportive relationships, and practicing mindfulness, we unlock the boundless reservoirs of resilience within ourselves, propelling us forward on the path to healing and flourishing. Remember that resilience is not the absence of adversity but rather the capacity to rise above it, emerging from the crucible of challenge stronger, wiser, and more resilient than before.

Part Three
Navigating Holistic Healing

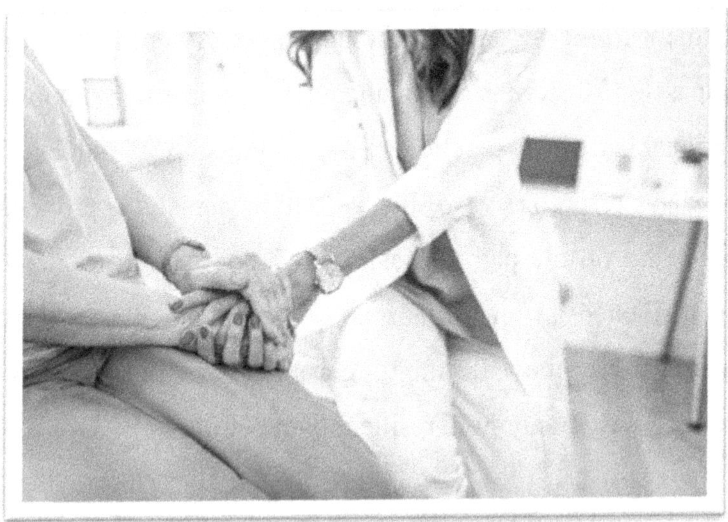

Healing the Body

In this chapter, we embark on a journey to explore holistic approaches to physical healing, recognizing the profound interconnectedness of mind, body, and spirit in the quest for wholeness. By addressing the physical manifestations of trauma through mindful nutrition, regular exercise, nurturing bodywork, and alternative therapies, we unlock the body's innate capacity for healing and restoration.

Nutrition:

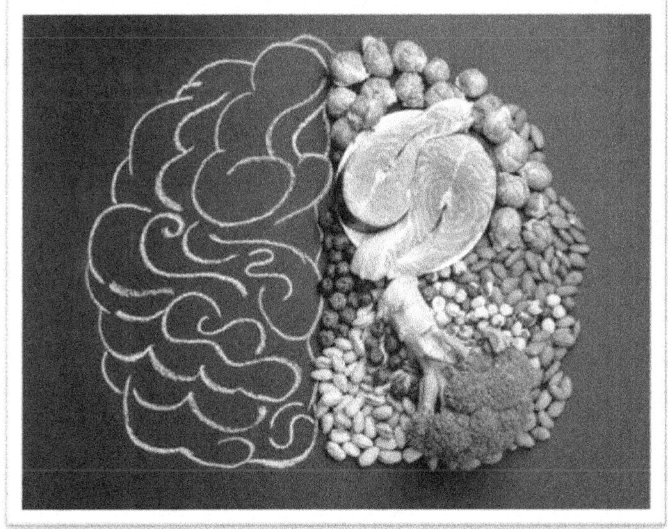

Nutrition serves as the cornerstone of physical well-being, exerting a profound influence on our overall health and resilience, especially in the aftermath of trauma. Embrace a diet rich in whole, nutrient-dense foods, including vibrant fruits, colorful vegetables, lean proteins, whole grains, and healthy fats. Prioritize foods that nourish and support your body's healing process, while minimizing processed foods, refined sugars, and artificial additives. Experiment with incorporating healing foods and herbs such as turmeric, ginger, garlic, and leafy greens into your meals to reduce inflammation, support immune function, and promote optimal health.

Example: Start your day with a nourishing breakfast bowl filled with antioxidant-rich berries, creamy Greek yogurt, crunchy nuts, and a sprinkle of cinnamon. Not only does it provide a delicious and energizing start to your day, but it also supports your body's healing process with a nutrient-packed boost.

Exercise:

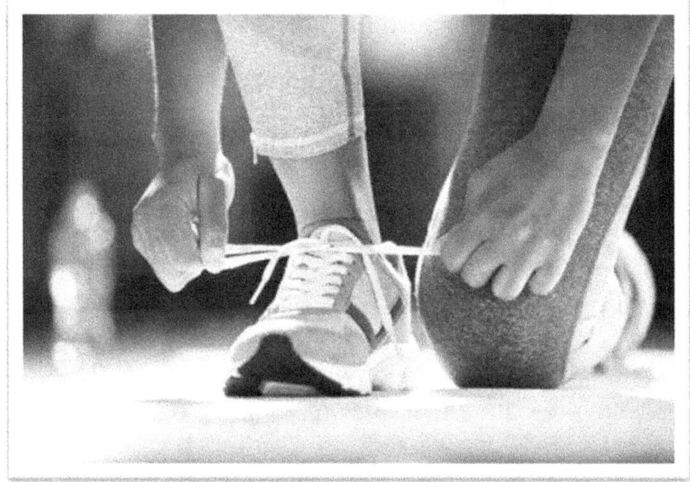

Regular physical activity is essential for promoting physical and emotional well-being and plays a vital role in healing from trauma. Engage in activities that bring you joy and vitality, whether it's brisk walking, jogging, swimming or practicing yoga. Exercise stimulates the release of endorphins, neurotransmitters that act as natural painkillers and mood elevators, while also promoting relaxation, stress reduction, and better sleep. Aim for at least 30 minutes of moderate-intensity exercise most days of the week, and remember that even small bursts of activity can have significant benefits for your physical and mental health.

Example: Invite a friend or family member to join you for a fun and energizing workout session at home or in a local studio. Not only does it provide an opportunity for social connection and laughter, but it also enhances your mood, boosts your energy levels, and supports your body's healing process.

Bodywork and Alternative Therapies:

Bodywork and alternative therapies offer holistic approaches to physical healing, addressing the body's natural ability to heal itself and promoting relaxation, stress reduction, and overall well-being. Explore modalities such as massage therapy, acupuncture, chiropractic care, Reiki, and aromatherapy to support your body's healing process and alleviate physical tension and discomfort. These therapies help release stored trauma from the body, improve circulation, and restore balance to the nervous system, facilitating deeper levels of healing and relaxation.

Example: Treat yourself to a rejuvenating massage or acupuncture session to release tension, reduce pain, and promote relaxation in your body. Alternatively, explore self-care practices such as foam rolling, stretching, or using essential oils for aromatherapy at home to support your body's healing journey.

Fun Exercise: Dance Therapy

Dance therapy harnesses the transformative power of movement and creative expression to promote healing, self-discovery, and emotional well-being. Put on your favorite music and allow yourself to move freely and intuitively, expressing yourself without judgment or inhibition.

Dance therapy can help release pent-up emotions, reduce anxiety, and cultivate a sense of joy, empowerment, and vitality. Experiment with different styles of dance, from salsa to hip-hop to ballet, and notice how each movement makes you feel physically, emotionally, and spiritually.

Hydration:

Proper hydration is essential for maintaining optimal physical and mental function, as well as supporting the body's natural detoxification processes. Drink plenty of water throughout the day to stay hydrated and replenish fluids lost through sweat, urination, and respiration. Aim to consume at least 8-10 glasses of water daily, adjusting your intake based on factors such as climate, activity level, and individual hydration needs.

Example: Keep a reusable water bottle with you throughout the day as a reminder to stay hydrated, and sip water regularly, especially during and after exercise or exposure to heat. Enhance the flavor and health benefits of your water by infusing it with slices of lemon, cucumber, mint, or berries.

Restorative Sleep:

Quality sleep is vital for physical healing, cognitive function, emotional regulation, and overall well-being. Prioritize restorative sleep by establishing a consistent sleep schedule, creating a relaxing bedtime routine, and optimizing your sleep environment for comfort and relaxation. Aim for 7-9 hours of uninterrupted sleep each night, allowing your body and mind to recharge, repair, and rejuvenate.

Example: Create a soothing bedtime ritual to signal to your body that it's time to unwind and prepare for sleep. Engage in calming activities such as reading, gentle stretching, or listening to calming music before bed, and avoid stimulating screens and caffeine in the hours leading up to bedtime. Create a comfortable sleep environment with a supportive mattress, soft bedding, and minimal distractions to promote deep, restorative sleep.

Nature Therapy:

Spending time in nature offers profound benefits for physical and emotional well-being, promoting relaxation, stress reduction, and healing. Engage in outdoor activities such as hiking, gardening, or simply taking leisurely walks in nature to connect with the natural world and replenish your spirit. Nature therapy can help reduce cortisol levels, boost mood, and enhance immune function, supporting your body's innate healing abilities.

Example: Dedicate time each week to immerse yourself in nature, whether it's exploring a nearby park, going for a nature walk, or spending time in your backyard garden. Take time to observe the sights, sounds, and sensations of the natural world, allowing yourself to relax and unwind in nature's embrace.

Mind-Body Practices:

Mind-body practices such as meditation, mindfulness, tai chi, and qigong offer powerful tools for promoting physical healing, reducing stress, and enhancing overall well-being. Incorporate these practices into your daily routine to cultivate relaxation, improve self-awareness, and foster a sense of connection between mind, body, and spirit. Explore different techniques and find the practices that resonate most with you, incorporating them into your life as tools for holistic healing and resilience.

Example: Dedicate a few minutes each day to mindfulness meditation, focusing on your breath and observing sensations in your body with gentle curiosity and acceptance. Alternatively, explore gentle movement practices such as tai chi or qigong to promote balance, flexibility, and energy flow throughout your body.

Herbal Remedies and Supplements:

Herbal remedies and supplements offer natural support for physical healing and overall well-being, providing essential nutrients, antioxidants, and medicinal properties to support the body's healing process. Explore herbal remedies such as herbal teas, tinctures, and supplements containing adaptogenic herbs, immune-supporting herbs, and anti-inflammatory botanicals to promote resilience, vitality, and longevity.

Example: Incorporate immune-boosting herbs such as echinacea, elderberry, and astragalus into your daily routine during times of increased stress or vulnerability. Brew a soothing cup of herbal tea with calming herbs such as chamomile, passionflower, or valerian root to promote relaxation and restful sleep.

Body Awareness Practices:

Cultivating body awareness through practices such as body scanning, breathwork, and somatic experiencing can deepen your connection with your body and facilitate physical healing. Pay attention to sensations, emotions, and areas of tension or discomfort in your body, allowing yourself to process and release stored trauma and stress. By developing greater body awareness, you empower yourself to listen to your body's cues and respond with compassion and care.

Example: Practice a body scan meditation, starting at the top of your head and slowly moving your awareness down through your body, observing sensations in each area with curiosity and nonjudgment. Notice any areas of tension or discomfort and breathe into them, allowing them to soften and release with each exhale.

By embracing holistic approaches to physical healing, including mindful nutrition, regular exercise, nurturing bodywork, and alternative therapies, we honor the body's wisdom and resilience on our journey towards wholeness and vitality. Remember to listen to your body's signals and honor its needs with compassion and care, incorporating practices that nourish and support your physical and emotional well-being. By prioritizing physical self-care, we lay a solid foundation for healing, resilience, and flourishing in all aspects of our lives.

Nurturing the Mind

In this chapter, we explore the profound impact of mental health practices on healing from trauma, emphasizing the importance of cultivating a nurturing and resilient mind. By incorporating practices such as mindfulness, meditation, therapy, and self-care into our daily lives, we empower ourselves to navigate the complexities of trauma with compassion, courage, and grace.

The Importance of Mental Health Practices:

Healing from trauma requires more than just addressing physical symptoms—it necessitates tending to the intricate landscape of the mind. Mental health practices provide essential tools for processing emotions, calming the nervous system, and cultivating resilience in the face of adversity. By prioritizing mental well-being, we create a foundation for healing that encompasses the entirety of our being, fostering a sense of wholeness and vitality.

Mindfulness:

Mindfulness is the practice of bringing focused attention to the present moment with openness, curiosity, and acceptance. Mindfulness allows us to observe our thoughts, emotions, and sensations without judgment, cultivating awareness and equanimity in the midst of life's challenges. Through mindfulness, we develop greater self-awareness, emotional regulation, and compassion for ourselves and others.

Example: Practice a simple mindfulness exercise by focusing on your breath for a few minutes each day. Sit comfortably in a quiet space, close your eyes, and bring your attention to the sensation of your breath as it enters and leaves your body. Notice the rise and fall of your chest or the sensation of air passing through your nostrils. Whenever your mind wanders, gently guide your attention back to your breath, cultivating a sense of presence and calm.

Meditation:

Meditation is a practice of training the mind to cultivate qualities such as concentration, clarity, and emotional balance. Through regular meditation practice, we develop greater insight into the workings of our minds and learn to relate to our thoughts and emotions with greater ease and equanimity. Meditation techniques vary widely, including mindfulness meditation, loving-kindness meditation, and body scan meditation, allowing for flexibility and adaptability to individual preferences and needs.

Example: Experiment with a loving-kindness meditation practice by silently repeating phrases such as "May I be happy, may I be healthy, may I be safe, may I be at ease." Extend these wishes of loving-kindness to yourself, then gradually expand them to include loved ones, acquaintances, and even difficult individuals. Notice the feelings of warmth and compassion that arise as you cultivate a sense of loving-kindness towards yourself and others.

Therapy:

Therapy provides a safe and supportive space for exploring and processing emotions, gaining insight into patterns of thought and behavior, and developing coping strategies for managing stress and trauma. Whether through individual therapy, group therapy, or specialized modalities such as cognitive-behavioral therapy (CBT), dialectical behavior therapy (DBT), or Eye Movement Desensitization and Reprocessing (EMDR), therapy offers invaluable support and guidance on the journey of healing.

Example: Consider seeking therapy with a licensed mental health professional who specializes in trauma-informed care. Together, you can explore the impact of trauma on your life, develop coping skills for managing symptoms, and cultivate a deeper understanding of yourself and your experiences. Therapy offers a collaborative partnership in healing, providing a compassionate space for growth and transformation.

Self-Care:

Self-care encompasses a wide range of practices and activities that nourish and replenish the mind, body, and spirit. Self-care involves honoring your needs, setting boundaries, and prioritizing activities that promote well-being and resilience. Whether it's engaging in hobbies, spending time in nature, connecting with loved ones, or practicing relaxation techniques, self-care is an essential component of maintaining mental health and fostering resilience.

Example: Create a self-care routine tailored to your unique needs and preferences. Dedicate time each day to engage in activities that bring you joy, relaxation, and fulfillment, whether it's reading a book, taking a bubble bath, or going for a leisurely walk in nature. Make self-care a priority in your life, recognizing that nurturing your well-being is essential for healing and resilience.

Expressive Arts Therapy:

Expressive arts therapy encompasses a variety of creative modalities, including visual arts, music, dance, writing, and drama, as vehicles for self-expression, exploration, and healing. Engaging in expressive arts activities allows individuals to bypass verbal communication barriers and access deeper layers of emotion and insight. Through the creative process, individuals can externalize their internal experiences, gain new perspectives, and integrate fragmented aspects of the self.

Example: Set aside time each week for creative expression through art, music, or writing. Allow yourself to explore different mediums and techniques without judgment, focusing on the process rather than the end result. Notice how engaging in creative activities helps to release tension, express emotions, and foster a sense of empowerment and self-discovery.

Breathwork:

Breathwork encompasses a variety of techniques that utilize conscious breathing patterns to promote relaxation, stress reduction, and emotional release. By harnessing the power of the breath, individuals can regulate their nervous system, access altered states of consciousness, and facilitate deep healing on physical, emotional, and spiritual levels. Breathwork techniques range from simple deep breathing exercises to more structured practices such as Holotropic Breathwork or Wim Hof Method.

Example: Try incorporating a simple deep breathing exercise into your daily routine as a tool for stress reduction and relaxation. Find a comfortable seated or lying position, close your eyes, and bring your awareness to your breath. Inhale deeply through your nose, allowing your abdomen to expand, then exhale slowly and completely through your mouth. Repeat this cycle of deep breathing for several minutes, noticing the calming effects on your body and mind.

Gratitude Practice:

Cultivating gratitude is a powerful mental health practice that can promote resilience, positivity, and emotional well-being. Gratitude involves intentionally focusing on the blessings, joys, and positive aspects of life, even amidst adversity. By shifting our attention towards gratitude, we reframe our perspective and cultivate a sense of abundance, appreciation, and connection with ourselves and the world around us.

Example: Start a gratitude journal and make it a daily habit to write down three things you are grateful for each day. These can be simple pleasures, moments of connection with others, or experiences of growth and learning. Reflect on your entries regularly, allowing yourself to savor the feelings of gratitude and abundance that arise, and notice how this practice shifts your mindset towards positivity and resilience.

Community Support:

Building connections with others and seeking support from a community can be an invaluable aspect of mental health and healing. Whether through support groups, online forums, or social networks, connecting with others who have shared experiences can provide validation, understanding, and a sense of belonging. Sharing stories, offering empathy, and receiving support from others can foster resilience and facilitate healing from trauma.

Example:

Join a support group or online community for individuals who have experienced similar traumatic events. Participate in group discussions, share your experiences, and offer support to

others in need. Connecting with a community of understanding and supportive individuals can help you feel less alone and provide valuable insights and perspectives on your healing journey.

Grounding Techniques:

Grounding techniques are strategies used to anchor oneself in the present moment and regulate overwhelming emotions or sensations. These techniques can help individuals feel more centered, calm, and connected to their bodies and surroundings. Examples of grounding techniques include deep breathing exercises, progressive muscle relaxation, sensory awareness exercises, and visualization techniques.

Example: Practice a simple grounding exercise by focusing on your senses. Take a few deep breaths and then notice five things you can see, four things you can touch, three things you can hear, two things you can smell, and one thing you can taste. This exercise helps bring your attention to the present moment and can be particularly helpful during moments of stress or anxiety.

Nurturing the mind is a transformative journey of self-discovery, healing, and empowerment—an invitation to cultivate resilience and well-being from the inside out. By incorporating mental health practices such as mindfulness, meditation, therapy, and self-care into our daily lives, we honor the complexity of our experiences and embrace the potential for growth and healing. Remember that healing is a nonlinear process, and each step we take towards nurturing our minds brings us closer to wholeness, vitality, and authenticity.

Reconnecting with Spirit

Examine the role of spirituality, connection, and purpose in the healing journey, offering guidance on finding meaning and reclaiming one's sense of self.

In this chapter, we embark on a journey to explore the profound role of spirituality, connection, and purpose in the process of healing from trauma. By delving into the depths of our inner selves and fostering a sense of connection with something greater than ourselves, we can discover meaning, purpose, and renewal on the path to wholeness. Through reflection, practice, and exploration, we invite the spirit to guide us towards healing, transformation, and reconnection with our authentic selves.

Understanding Spirituality:

Spirituality is a deeply personal journey that involves exploring our innermost essence, acknowledging our interconnectedness with all beings, and seeking meaning, purpose, and transcendence in life. It transcends religious affiliations, embracing a universal quest for understanding, peace, and connection with the divine or sacred within and around us. Spirituality offers a framework for navigating life's challenges, finding solace in times of suffering, and nurturing a sense of connection with something greater than ourselves.

Example: Begin a daily practice of meditation or prayer, setting aside a few moments each day to connect with your inner self and the divine presence within you. Allow yourself to quiet your mind, open your heart, and listen to the whispers of your soul, trusting in the guidance and wisdom that emerges.

Finding Meaning and Purpose:

Finding meaning and purpose in the aftermath of trauma is a transformative process that empowers us to reclaim agency and resilience in our lives. By reframing our experiences through the lens of meaning-making, we discover the hidden gifts and lessons embedded within our journey, guiding us towards a sense of purpose and fulfillment. Through reflection, introspection, and exploration, we uncover the unique contributions we can make to the world and the legacy we wish to leave behind.

Example: Reflect on the experiences that have shaped your life, considering how they have influenced your values, beliefs, and aspirations. Identify moments of growth, resilience, or insight that have emerged from your journey, and contemplate how you can use these experiences to contribute to the greater good or pursue meaningful goals in your life.

Cultivating Connection:

Connection is essential for healing from trauma, offering a sense of belonging, support, and understanding in our lives. Cultivating connections with ourselves, others, and the world around us helps to counteract feelings of isolation, disconnection, and alienation, restoring a sense of wholeness and belonging in our lives. Whether through nurturing relationships, engaging in acts of service, or connecting with nature, we deepen our capacity for healing and growth.

Example: Reach out to a trusted friend, family member, or support group and share your experiences, thoughts, and feelings with them. Allow yourself to be vulnerable and open to receiving support and understanding from others, knowing that you are not alone on your journey. Notice how connecting with others helps to alleviate feelings of isolation and reinforces your sense of belonging and worthiness.

Expressive Arts Therapy:

Expressive arts therapy offers a creative avenue for exploring and processing emotions, tapping into our inner wisdom, and fostering self-expression and healing. Whether through visual arts, music, dance, writing, or drama, expressive arts allow us to bypass verbal communication barriers and access deeper layers of emotion and *insight.*

Example: Set aside time each week for creative expression through art, music, or writing. Allow yourself to explore different mediums and techniques without judgment, focusing on the process rather than the end result. Notice how engaging in creative activities helps to release tension, express emotions, and foster a sense of empowerment and self-discovery.

Prayer:

Prayer is a powerful spiritual practice that offers a direct line of communication with the divine or sacred. Whether through spoken words, silent contemplation, or heartfelt intentions, prayer provides an opportunity to express gratitude, seek guidance, and cultivate a deeper connection with the divine presence within and around us. Prayer can be personalized to align with one's beliefs, values, and spiritual tradition, serving as a source of comfort, strength, and inspiration on the journey of healing and transformation.

Example: Set aside dedicated time each day for prayer, either in the morning to set intentions for the day ahead or in the evening for reflection and gratitude. Create a sacred space where you feel comfortable and at peace, and engage in prayer practices that resonate with your heart and soul. Allow yourself to speak from the depths of your being, expressing your hopes, fears, gratitude, and aspirations with sincerity and trust in the divine presence.

Giving and Acts of Service:

Giving and acts of service are powerful ways to express compassion, generosity, and interconnectedness with others. By extending kindness, support, and resources to those in need, we not only alleviate suffering and promote well-being in others but also cultivate a sense of purpose, fulfillment, and connection within ourselves. Giving can take many forms, including volunteering, donating to charity, offering a listening ear, or performing random acts of kindness, each serving as an opportunity to embody the spirit of love and compassion in action.

Example: Identify a cause or organization that aligns with your values and interests, and find ways to contribute your time, skills, or resources to support their mission. Whether it's volunteering at a local shelter, organizing a fundraiser, or participating in a community service project, find opportunities to give back and make a positive impact in the lives of others. Notice how acts of service not only benefit those you serve but also bring joy, fulfillment, and a sense of connection to your own life.

Forgiveness Practice:

Forgiveness is a transformative spiritual practice that involves letting go of resentment, anger, and blame towards ourselves and others. By cultivating forgiveness, we release the emotional burdens of the past, liberate ourselves from suffering, and open our hearts to healing, reconciliation, and compassion. Forgiveness does not condone harmful behavior but rather empowers us to reclaim our power and freedom by choosing love and compassion over resentment and bitterness.

Example: Practice forgiveness by writing a letter to yourself or someone who has hurt you, expressing your feelings, and offering forgiveness from a place of compassion and understanding. Alternatively, engage in loving-kindness meditation, directing wishes of forgiveness towards yourself, others, and all beings, embracing the transformative power of compassion and reconciliation.

Gratitude Circle:

A gratitude circle is a group practice where individuals come together to express gratitude, share blessings, and cultivate a sense of appreciation and abundance in their lives. By gathering in community and acknowledging the blessings and gifts we have received, we amplify the energy of gratitude, deepen our sense of connection with others, and foster a collective spirit of joy, generosity, and love.

Example: Organize a gratitude circle with friends, family members, or colleagues, either in person or virtually. Create a sacred space where everyone can gather comfortably, and take turns sharing something they are grateful for, whether big or small. Listen attentively to each person's sharing, and offer words of affirmation, encouragement, or support, fostering a sense of unity, appreciation, and connection within the group.

Mindful Reflection:

Mindful reflection is a contemplative practice that involves pausing, observing, and exploring our inner thoughts, emotions, and experiences with awareness and compassion. Through mindful reflection, we create space for self-inquiry, self-awareness, and self-discovery, allowing us to deepen our understanding of ourselves, our relationships, and our place in the world. Mindful reflection can take many forms, including journaling, meditation, or silent contemplation, each offering a pathway to greater clarity, insight, and spiritual growth.

Example: Set aside time each day for mindful reflection, either in the morning to set intentions for the day ahead or in the evening for self-examination and review. Find a quiet and comfortable space where you can be alone with your thoughts, and engage in practices such as journaling, meditation, or mindfulness exercises. Allow yourself to observe your thoughts and emotions with curiosity and nonjudgment, embracing whatever arises with acceptance and compassion.

Reconnecting with spirit is a transformative journey of self-discovery, healing, and renewal—an invitation to explore the depths of our inner selves and embrace the sacredness of life itself. By cultivating spirituality, finding meaning and purpose, and nurturing connections with ourselves, others, and the world around us, we open ourselves to the possibility of healing, growth, and transformation. Trust in your inner wisdom, follow your heart's guidance, and embrace the sacredness of your own healing journey.

Part Four
Integrating Healing Practices

The Healing Journey in Action

In this chapter, we celebrate the inspiring stories of individuals who have courageously embarked on the journey of healing from trauma and transformed their lives through holistic healing practices. By sharing their experiences, insights, and triumphs, we offer hope, encouragement, and guidance to those navigating their own healing journey. Through real-life examples and practical exercises, we illuminate the transformative power of holistic healing and inspire others to embrace the path of healing and self-discovery.

The Power of Personal Stories:

Personal stories are powerful vehicles for inspiration, empathy, and connection—they provide glimpses into the human experience, offering validation, understanding, and hope to those who may be struggling. By sharing stories of resilience, courage, and transformation, we shine a light on the inherent capacity for healing and growth within each individual, empowering others to believe in their own potential for healing and renewal.

Exercise:
Read or listen to personal stories of trauma survivors who have undergone transformative healing journeys. Reflect on the themes, challenges, and insights shared by these individuals, and notice how their stories resonate with your own experiences and aspirations for healing. Consider journaling about the emotions, thoughts, and reflections that arise as you engage with these stories, allowing them to inspire and guide you on your own healing journey.

Case Studies of Holistic Healing

Below are two case studies illustrating how individuals have overcome trauma and transformed their lives through holistic healing practices:

Case Study 1: Sarah's Journey of Self-Compassion

Sarah experienced childhood trauma that left her struggling with anxiety, depression, and low self-esteem in adulthood. Through therapy, Sarah learned to cultivate self-compassion, recognizing that she was not to blame for her past experiences and that she deserved love, acceptance, and healing. Sarah incorporated mindfulness meditation, journaling, and creative expression into her daily routine, allowing herself to explore and process her emotions with kindness and curiosity. Over time, Sarah experienced profound shifts in her self-perception and began to embrace her inner strength, resilience, and worthiness. Today, Sarah leads a fulfilling life, empowered by her journey of self-compassion and holistic healing.

Example Exercise: Practice self-compassion by writing a compassionate letter to yourself, acknowledging the challenges you have faced and expressing kindness, understanding, and support towards yourself. Reflect on the qualities, strengths, and resilience that have emerged from your journey, and affirm your worthiness of love, healing, and happiness.

Case Study 2: Mark's Journey of Mindful Awareness

Mark struggled with PTSD following a traumatic experience during his military service. Seeking relief from his symptoms, Mark turned to mindfulness meditation as a means of calming his mind and regulating his emotions. Through consistent practice, Mark learned to observe his thoughts, sensations, and emotions with mindful awareness, allowing them to arise and pass without judgment or attachment. As Mark cultivated greater presence and acceptance in the present moment, he experienced a reduction in his PTSD symptoms and an increased sense of peace and well-being. Today, Mark continues to incorporate mindfulness into his daily life, finding solace and strength in the practice of mindful awareness.

Example Exercise: Practice mindfulness meditation by sitting quietly and bringing your attention to your breath, sensations, or surroundings. Notice the thoughts, emotions, and sensations that arise without trying to change or control them. Allow yourself to simply observe and experience each moment with curiosity and openness, cultivating a sense of presence and acceptance in the here and now.

Peer Support Networks:

Peer support networks play a crucial role in the healing journey, providing individuals with a sense of belonging, understanding, and validation. By connecting with others who have experienced similar struggles, individuals can find empathy, encouragement, and practical guidance on their healing path. Peer support groups, online communities, and mentorship programs offer opportunities for individuals to share their stories, offer support, and learn from one another's experiences.

Example Exercise: Seek out a peer support group or online community focused on healing from trauma. Participate in group discussions, share your experiences, and offer support to others in need. Notice how connecting with peers who have walked a similar path can provide validation, understanding, and a sense of solidarity on your healing journey.

Integration of Holistic Modalities:

Holistic healing involves integrating a variety of modalities and approaches that address the interconnected aspects of mind, body, and spirit. From therapy and counseling to mindfulness practices, creative expression, and body-based therapies, individuals can explore a range of holistic modalities to support their healing journey. By adopting a comprehensive and personalized approach to healing, individuals can address the diverse dimensions of their well-being and cultivate resilience, empowerment, and wholeness.

Example Exercise: Create a holistic healing plan that incorporates a variety of modalities tailored to your unique needs and preferences. Include practices such as therapy, mindfulness meditation, yoga, art therapy, and nutrition counseling, among others. Experiment with different modalities and observe how each contributes to your overall well-being and healing process.

Cultivation of Gratitude and Resilience:

Cultivating gratitude and resilience are foundational practices that support individuals in navigating the challenges of the healing journey with grace and strength. By cultivating gratitude for the blessings, joys, and lessons in life, individuals can shift their perspective towards abundance and resilience, fostering a sense of hope, positivity, and empowerment. Through resilience-building practices such as self-care, boundary-setting, and positive coping strategies, individuals can strengthen their capacity to overcome adversity and thrive in the face of challenges.

Example Exercise: Start a gratitude journal and make it a daily practice to write down three things you are grateful for each day.

Additionally, identify one resilient action you can take each day to nurture your well-being and cope with stressors effectively. Notice how these practices enhance your sense of gratitude, resilience, and overall well-being over time.

Creating Your Holistic Healing Plan

Welcome to the chapter that will guide you through crafting your personalized holistic healing plan, tailored to your unique needs and circumstances. By integrating various holistic modalities and practices, you'll embark on a transformative journey towards resilience, empowerment, and well-being. Get ready to explore the depths of holistic health and wellness and take control of your healing journey.

Step 1: Self-Assessment and Reflection

Begin by delving into a deep reflection of your current state of being. Consider all aspects of your life—physical, emotional, mental, and spiritual. Examine your past experiences, identifying challenges and strengths. This self-awareness lays the foundation for understanding your needs and setting intentions for healing.

Example Exercise:
  o Allocate dedicated time for introspection, perhaps 30 minutes to an hour.
  o Utilize journaling as a tool for self-reflection, jotting down thoughts, emotions, and insights.
  o Identify recurring patterns or triggers contributing to your challenges.

Step 2: Identify Holistic Modalities and Practices

Cast a wide net as you explore various holistic modalities and practices. From therapy and meditation to yoga and nutrition, there's a plethora of options to consider. Research each modality to understand its principles and benefits, discerning what resonates most deeply with your healing journey.

Example Exercise:
  o Create a list of holistic modalities and practices that intrigue you.
  o Investigate each modality further through books, online resources, or consultations.
  o Attend introductory workshops or classes to gain firsthand experience and insight.

Step 3: Develop Your Healing Plan

With insights from your self-assessment and exploration, it's time to craft your personalized healing plan. Define specific practices, goals, and actionable steps that align with your aspirations for well-being. Flexibility is key—allow your plan to evolve organically as you progress on your journey.

Example Healing Plan:
- o *Daily:* Dedicate 20 minutes to mindfulness meditation, followed by journaling and a gratitude practice.
- o *Weekly:* Attend therapy sessions and yoga classes, engaging in creative expression through writing or art.
- o *Monthly:* Treat yourself to bodywork sessions like massage or acupuncture, and participate in wellness retreats for deeper exploration.

Step 4: Implement and Evaluate Your Plan

Now comes the crucial step of putting your healing plan into action. Incorporate your chosen practices into your daily routine, utilizing reminders and accountability measures to stay on track. Regularly assess your plan's effectiveness, making adjustments as needed based on your evolving needs and experiences.

Example Exercise:

Visualize your healing plan using a vision board or mind map, fostering clarity and motivation.

Set up reminders on your devices or enlist a supportive friend to help keep you accountable.

Maintain a journal to track your progress, insights, and any shifts in your well-being.

Congratulations on taking the proactive steps towards creating your personalized holistic healing plan. By integrating self-assessment, exploration, and intentional action, you're empowering yourself to embark on a transformative journey towards holistic health and wellness. Embrace the process with patience and trust, knowing that you hold the power to cultivate resilience, empowerment, and well-being in your life. Your journey towards wholeness begins now—embrace it wholeheartedly.

Conclusion
Triumph over Trauma

A Journey to Wholeness

In this final chapter, we celebrate the remarkable journey of triumph over trauma and the profound transformation that occurs when individuals embrace holistic healing. Through the stories of courage, resilience, and growth shared throughout this book, we witness the transformative power of holistic approaches in overcoming adversity and achieving true holistic health and wellness. As we reflect on the lessons learned and the tools acquired, we affirm our commitment to living wholeheartedly and embracing the journey towards wholeness.

Celebrating Transformative Journeys:

Throughout this book, we have explored the multifaceted nature of trauma and the diverse pathways to healing that individuals embark upon. We've witnessed stories of resilience, perseverance, and triumph—testaments to the human spirit's capacity for growth and transformation in the face of adversity. From cultivating mindfulness and self-compassion to embracing spirituality and connection, individuals have harnessed the power of holistic healing to reclaim their lives and thrive.

Example: Reflect on the stories shared in this book, identifying common themes, insights, and moments of inspiration that resonated with you. Consider how these stories have impacted your own understanding of trauma and healing, and celebrate the courage and resilience demonstrated by the individuals who have shared their journeys with honesty and vulnerability.

Embracing Holistic Health and Wellness:

Holistic healing encompasses more than just the absence of symptoms—it embodies a state of balance, harmony, and well-being in all aspects of life. By addressing the interconnected dimensions of mind, body, and spirit, individuals can cultivate resilience, empowerment, and vitality on their healing journey. From practicing self-care and setting boundaries to nurturing relationships and finding purpose, holistic health and wellness are rooted in self-awareness, self-compassion, and self-discovery.

Exercise: Create a vision board or collage that represents your vision of holistic health and wellness. Include images, words, and symbols that reflect the qualities, values, and aspirations you associate with living a balanced and fulfilling life. Display your vision board in a prominent place where you can see it daily, allowing it to serve as a source of inspiration and motivation on your journey towards wholeness.

Embracing the Journey Towards Wholeness:

The journey towards wholeness is not a destination but a lifelong process of growth, discovery, and self-compassion. It requires courage to face the shadows of the past, resilience to navigate the challenges of the present, and faith to trust in the possibilities of the future. As we embrace the journey towards wholeness, we honor our experiences, cultivate self-acceptance, and embrace the fullness of our humanity with grace and gratitude.

Example: Take a moment to reflect on your own journey towards wholeness, acknowledging the progress you've made, the challenges you've overcome, and the growth you've experienced along the way. Celebrate your resilience, courage, and commitment to healing, knowing that every step you take brings you closer to living authentically and wholeheartedly.

Reflection on Growth and Transformation:

Take time to reflect on your personal growth and transformation throughout your healing journey. Consider the challenges you've faced, the lessons you've learned, and the strengths you've discovered within yourself. Celebrate your progress and acknowledge the resilience and courage it took to overcome adversity and embrace healing.

Commitment to Self-Compassion:

Make a commitment to practice self-compassion and self-care as you navigate the ups and downs of life's journey. Be gentle with yourself, acknowledge your humanity, and embrace imperfection with kindness and understanding. Cultivate a loving and nurturing relationship with yourself, knowing that you are worthy of compassion, care, and acceptance.

Gratitude Practice:

Cultivate a practice of gratitude as you reflect on the journey of trauma triumphs and holistic healing. Express gratitude for the support, resources, and opportunities that have contributed to your healing journey. Recognize the blessings and lessons

that have emerged from your experiences, fostering a sense of appreciation and abundance in your life.

Integration of Learnings:

Integrate the learnings and insights gained from this book into your daily life and healing practice. Incorporate holistic healing modalities, self-care practices, and mindfulness techniques that resonate with you, empowering yourself to continue the journey towards wholeness and well-being.

Connection and Community:

Seek out connections and community support to enrich your healing journey. Surround yourself with individuals who uplift and empower you, sharing your experiences, insights, and challenges with trusted friends, family members, or support groups. Draw strength from the collective wisdom and compassion of those who walk alongside you on the path to wholeness.

As we conclude our exploration of trauma triumphs and the journey to wholeness, let us carry forward the lessons learned, the wisdom gained, and the compassion cultivated on this transformative journey. May we continue to embrace holistic healing as a pathway to reclaiming our lives, nurturing our well-being, and living with authenticity, purpose, and joy. And may we never forget the resilience, strength, and beauty that reside within each of us, guiding us towards the light of wholeness and the triumph of the human spirit.

Congratulations

Congratulations on completing this transformative journey! Your dedication to healing trauma and embracing holistic well-being is commendable and inspiring. As you close this chapter, remember your resilience and trust in your inner wisdom. Continue cultivating compassion and resilience, knowing you're not alone on this journey. May you find continued growth and healing, supported by your inner strength and the community around you. With each step forward, may you discover deeper levels of peace, joy, and fulfillment. Embrace the journey ahead with courage and openness, knowing that you have the power to create a life filled with love and abundance.

Resources: Worksheets and Action Plans

Worksheet I: Daily Mindfulness Practice Tracker

Instructions:

Use this worksheet to track your daily mindfulness practice and reflect on your experiences. Set aside a few minutes each day to complete the tracker and jot down any observations or insights.

Daily Mindfulness Practice Tracker

Date:..

....

Morning Mindfulness Meditation:

[Insert Duration]...

....

[Rate Your Experience: 1-10]:

....

....

Midday Mindful Moment:

[Insert Activity]:

....

....

[Rate Your Experience: 1-10]:

....

Evening Reflection:

[Write down any thoughts, feelings, or observations that arose during your mindfulness practice.]

....

....

....

Additional Notes:

[Record any challenges, successes, or adjustments you made to your mindfulness practice.]

....

....

....

....

Worksheet II: Gratitude Journal

Instructions:

Use this worksheet to cultivate a daily gratitude practice and enhance your well-being. Each day, take a few moments to reflect on the things you're grateful for and write them down in the journal.

Gratitude Journal
Date: ....   Three Things I'm Grateful For Today: [Write down one thing you're grateful for.   ....   [Write down another thing you're grateful for.]   ....

[Write down a third thing you're grateful for.]

....

....

....

Reflections:

[Take a moment to reflect on how expressing gratitude makes you feel. Notice any shifts in your mood or perspective.]

....

....

....

....

Additional Notes:

[Record any additional thoughts, feelings, or experiences related to your gratitude practice.]

....

....

....

These worksheets provide practical tools for readers to implement mindfulness practices and gratitude journaling in their daily lives, fostering greater self-awareness, well-being, and resilience.

Worksheet III: Values Clarification Exercise

Instructions:

Use this worksheet to explore your core values and beliefs, guiding you towards greater alignment with your authentic self and spiritual journey. Take your time to reflect on each prompt and write down your responses.

Core Values Identification:

Reflect on the values that are most important to you in life. Consider qualities or principles that you hold dear and strive to embody in your actions and decisions. Write down at least five core values that resonate with you.

Reflective Questions:

Answer the following questions to deepen your understanding of your core values and their significance in your life:

o What do your chosen core values mean to you personally?

- o How do these values influence your daily thoughts, behaviors, and interactions with others?
- o In what ways do you currently live in alignment with your core values? Are there areas where you feel out of alignment?
- o How do your core values contribute to your sense of purpose, fulfillment, and connection to something greater than yourself?

Values Integration:

- o Explore ways to integrate your core values into your daily life and spiritual practice.
- o Brainstorm actionable steps and commitments that align with each of your chosen values.
- o Write down specific goals or intentions for incorporating these values into your routine.

Reflection and Commitment:

- o Take a moment to reflect on the insights gained from this exercise.
- o Notice any shifts in your awareness, perspective, or sense of purpose.

- o Commit to living in alignment with your core values and honoring the wisdom of your spiritual journey.

Example:

Core values	Answers to Reflective Questions	Value integration
Compassion	Compassion means showing kindness and empathy towards myself and others, fostering understanding and acceptance in all interactions.	Practice acts of kindness and compassion towards myself and others daily.
Authenticity	Authenticity involves living in alignment with my true self, expressing my beliefs and values authentically without fear of judgment or rejection.	Express myself authentically in conversations and interactions, speaking my truth with integrity and vulnerability.

Connection	Connection is the sense of belonging and interconnection with all living beings, recognizing the inherent unity and oneness of the universe.	Cultivate deeper connections with loved ones through quality time, active listening, and heartfelt communication.
Gratitude	Gratitude is the practice of acknowledging and appreciating the blessings and lessons present in each moment, cultivating a sense of abundance and contentment.	Cultivate a daily gratitude practice, reflecting on three things I'm grateful for each day.
Growth	Growth entails embracing challenges and opportunities for learning and expansion, continuously evolving	Commit to personal and spiritual growth through self-reflection, learning, and exploration of new experiences and perspectives.

	and evolving on my spiritual journey.	
Reflection and Commitment: I commit to living in alignment with my core values of compassion, authenticity, connection, gratitude, and growth, integrating them into my daily life and spiritual practice. I trust that honoring these values will guide me on a path of greater meaning, purpose, and fulfillment in my journey of reconnecting with spirit.		

This worksheet provides readers with a structured framework for exploring their core values, aligning them with their spiritual journey, and committing to intentional action towards greater alignment and fulfillment.

Worksheet IV: Body Awareness and Self-Care Plan

Instructions:

Use this worksheet to deepen your body awareness and develop a personalized self-care plan to support your physical healing journey. Take your time to reflect on each prompt and write down your responses.

Body Scan Exercise:

Take a few moments to close your eyes and bring your attention to your body. Notice any areas of tension, discomfort, or relaxation. Starting from your head, slowly scan down to your toes, paying attention to each part of your body. Write down any sensations or observations that arise.

Reflective Questions:

Answer the following questions to explore your relationship with your body and identify areas for improvement in your self-care routine:

- o How do you currently prioritize self-care and physical well-being in your daily life?

- What physical symptoms or discomforts do you frequently experience? How do these symptoms impact your quality of life?
- Are there any areas of your body that you tend to neglect or ignore? What emotions or beliefs are associated with these areas?
- What activities or practices bring you joy, relaxation, and rejuvenation? How can you incorporate more of these activities into your self-care routine?

Self-Care Plan Development:

- Based on your reflections, brainstorm specific self-care practices and activities that address your physical needs and promote overall well-being.
- Write down actionable steps and commitments for each area of your body that requires attention.

Integration and Commitment:

- Reflect on the self-care practices and commitments outlined in your plan.
- Notice any resistance or barriers that arise and explore ways to overcome them.

o Commit to prioritizing your physical well-being and honoring your body's needs with compassion and intention.

Example: Body scan exercise

Body Scan Exercise:		
o Notice tension in shoulders from stress. o Tightness in lower back from sitting too long. o Lightness and relaxation in hands and feet.		
Reflective questions	Answers	Self-care plan development
How do you currently prioritize self-care and physical well-being in your daily life?	I prioritize self-care by incorporating daily walks and healthy meals, but I often neglect stretching and relaxation practices. joy and relaxation, but I don't make	Commit to incorporating daily stretching and relaxation exercises to alleviate tension and promote flexibility.

	time for them regularly.	
What physical symptoms or discomforts do you frequently experience? How do these symptoms impact your quality of life?	Frequent headaches and digestive issues impact my daily life and productivity.	Schedule regular breaks throughout the day to stretch and move, especially during long periods of sitting.
Are there any areas of your body that you tend to neglect or ignore? What emotions or beliefs are associated with these areas?	I tend to ignore discomfort in my lower back and avoid addressing it due to fear of aggravating the pain.	Explore holistic therapies such as massage or acupuncture to address chronic pain and discomfort in the lower back.
What activities or practices bring you joy, relaxation, and rejuvenation? How can you incorporate more of these	Activities like yoga, gardening, and spending time in nature bring me joy and relaxation, but I don't make	Prioritize outdoor activities like hiking, gardening, or picnicking on weekends to reconnect with

activities into your self-care routine?	time for them regularly.	nature and rejuvenate the body and mind.

Integration and Commitment:

I commit to prioritizing my physical well-being and incorporating self-care practices that honor my body's needs and promote overall health and vitality. I acknowledge that self-care is an essential aspect of my healing journey and commit to approaching it with compassion, consistency, and intention.

This worksheet empowers readers to deepen their body awareness, identify areas for improvement in their self-care routine, and develop actionable steps to support their physical healing journey.

Worksheet V: Action Plan for Personal Growth and Transformation

Instructions:

Use this worksheet to outline actionable steps and goals for personal growth and transformation on your healing journey. Take time to reflect on each suggestion and write down your responses.

Reflection on Current State:

- o Reflect on your current state of being and identify areas for personal growth and transformation.
- o Consider your strengths, challenges, and aspirations for the future.
- o Write down any insights or observations that arise.

Goal Setting:

- o Set specific, measurable, and achievable goals for personal growth and transformation.
- o Break down each goal into smaller, manageable steps or milestones.

o   Write down your goals and action steps for each area of focus.

Resources and Support:

o   Identify resources and support systems that will help you achieve your goals. This could include books, workshops, mentors, support groups, or holistic practitioners.

o   Write down any resources or support systems you plan to utilize.

Accountability and Tracking:

o   Establish accountability measures and tracking mechanisms to monitor your progress towards your goals. This could include setting deadlines, scheduling regular check-ins with a friend or mentor, or using a journal to track your achievements.

o   Write down your accountability measures and tracking methods.

Example:

Reflection on current state	Goal-setting	Resources and support	Accountability and tracking
I feel stuck in my current job and crave more fulfillment and purpose in my career.	Career: Explore alternative career paths and job opportunities aligned with my passions and values. Action steps: Research potential career options, update resume and LinkedIn profile, attend networking events.	Books: "The Power of Now" by Eckhart Tolle, "Daring Greatly" by Brené Brown	Set a deadline to apply for at least three new job opportunities within the next month.
I struggle with low self-esteem and negative	Self-Esteem: Practice self-love and positive affirmations to	Workshops: Self-compassion workshop at local	Use a journal to track daily gratitude practices, positive

self-talk, which hinders my ability to pursue my passions and dreams.	boost self-esteem and overcome limiting beliefs. Action steps: Start a daily gratitude journal, challenge negative thoughts with positive affirmations, seek therapy or counseling for additional support.	wellness center, Career exploration seminar at community college	affirmations, and reflections on personal growth and transformation.
I have a strong desire to cultivate more meaningful connections and	Relationships: Cultivate deeper connections with friends and family by prioritizing quality time	Mentor: Reach out to a trusted friend or family member who has successfull	Schedule weekly check-ins with a close friend or mentor to discuss progress towards career

relationships in my life.	and open communication. Action steps: Schedule regular social activities, initiate heart-to-heart conversations with loved ones, join a support group or community organization.	y navigated career transitions for guidance and support	and personal development goals.

Congratulations!

You've created a personalized action plan for personal growth and transformation that will guide you on your healing journey. By setting clear goals, utilizing resources and support, and establishing accountability measures, you're empowering yourself to take proactive steps towards a more fulfilling and meaningful life. Stay committed to your goals, be patient with yourself, and trust in the process of growth and transformation. Your journey towards healing and wholeness begins now.

Worksheet VI: Journal Ideas for Cultivating Awareness

o   Reflect on a recent experience that triggered strong emotions for you. What thoughts, sensations, and emotions did you notice in your body during this experience?

o   Describe a recurring pattern or behavior in your life that you would like to explore further. How does this pattern relate to past experiences or traumas?

o   Consider a challenging relationship or interaction in your life. What emotions arise when you think about this relationship? How do these emotions manifest in your body?

o   Explore moments of resistance or avoidance in your life. What thoughts or beliefs underlie these patterns of resistance? How do they influence your behavior and choices?

o   Reflect on a time when you felt a sense of calm and inner peace. What factors contributed to this feeling of well-being? How can you cultivate more moments of calm and presence in your daily life?

o   Explore a recent challenge or setback in your life. What thoughts, emotions, and physical sensations arise when you think about this experience? How does this challenge relate to your past experiences or beliefs about yourself?

o   Reflect on a positive coping strategy or resource that has helped you navigate difficult times. How does this strategy support your emotional well-being? How can you cultivate more of this resource in your life?

o   Consider a limiting belief or negative self-talk pattern that holds you back from fully embracing your potential. What evidence do you have to challenge this belief? How can you reframe it into a more empowering perspective?

o   Explore the concept of self-compassion and its role in healing from trauma. How do you typically respond to yourself in moments of pain or difficulty? How can you cultivate greater self-compassion and kindness towards yourself?

o   Reflect on moments of growth and resilience in your life. What strengths, qualities, or skills have you developed as a result of overcoming adversity? How can you draw upon these strengths to navigate future challenges?

Worksheet VII: Trauma trigger identification and management guide

Here are some prompts to help you identify and manage trauma triggers:

Identify Triggers:

- Think back to past traumatic experiences. What specific events, situations, or stimuli tend to bring up memories or emotions associated with those experiences?
- Are there certain sounds, smells, or sensations that trigger distressing memories or physical reactions?
- Do certain places or environments remind you of the traumatic event?
- Are there specific people or types of interactions that evoke feelings of fear, anxiety, or distress?

List Triggers:

- Identify and write down each trigger you have identified.
- Describe how each trigger makes you feel or what memories it brings up.
- Be specific and detailed in your descriptions to increase awareness of your triggers and their impact.

Develop Coping Strategies:

- o Brainstorm strategies for managing each trigger when it arises.
- o Consider relaxation techniques such as deep breathing, progressive muscle relaxation, or mindfulness exercises.
- o Think about distraction techniques like engaging in a favorite hobby or activity, listening to music, or focusing on your senses.
- o Reflect on how you have coped with triggers in the past and what has been effective for you.

Create a Support Plan:

- o Identify trusted friends, family members, or mental health professionals who can offer support when you are triggered.
- o Communicate your triggers and coping strategies to these individuals so they can provide assistance when needed.
- o Consider joining a support group or seeking therapy to connect with others who have experienced similar trauma.

Practice Self-Care:

- o Prioritize self-care practices that promote emotional and physical well-being.
- o Make time for activities that bring you joy, relaxation, and fulfillment.
- o Pay attention to your physical health by getting enough sleep, eating nutritious foods, and exercising regularly.
- o Be gentle with yourself and practice self-compassion as you navigate triggers and work towards healing and recovery.

Further Reading:

Banitt, S. P. (2012). The trauma tool kit: Healing PTSD from the inside out. Quest Books.

Freyd, J. J., & DePrince, A. P. (2013). Trauma and cognitive science: A meeting of minds, science, and human experience. Routledge.

Nemeroff, C. B., Bremner, J. D., Foa, E. B., Mayberg, H. S., North, C. S., & Stein, M. B. (2006). Posttraumatic stress disorder: a state-of-the-science review. Journal of psychiatric research, 40(1), 1-21.

Pack, M. (2016). Self-help for Trauma Therapists: A Practitioner's Guide. Routledge.

Scott, J. G., Warber, S. L., Dieppe, P., Jones, D., & Stange, K. C. (2017). Healing journey: a qualitative analysis of the healing experiences of Americans suffering from trauma and illness. BMJ open, 7(8), e016771.

Van der Merwe, C. N. (2009). Narrating our healing: Perspectives on working through trauma. Cambridge Scholars Publishing.

Wilkinson, M. (2017). Mind, brain and body. Healing trauma: the way forward. Journal of Analytical Psychology, 62(4), 526-543.

NOTES

NOTES

NOTES

NOTES

NOTES

NOTES

NOTES

NOTES